ARTIFICIAL INTELEGENCE IN CONSTRUCTION

THE FUTURE OF PROJECT MANAGEMENT

MICHAEL FURRY

Artificial Intelligence in Construction: The
Future of Project Management

Table Of Contents

Glossary

Definition of Key Terms and Concepts

References

List of Sources Cited in the Book

Introduction

Definition of Artificial Intelligence

Artificial Intelligence (AI) is a branch of computer science that emphasizes the creation of intelligent machines that can work and think like humans. The term AI was coined in the mid-1950s by John McCarthy, who is one of the founding fathers of the field. AI is a broad term that encompasses various sub-disciplines such as machine learning, natural language processing, robotics, and computer vision.

At its core, AI involves the development of algorithms that enable machines to learn from data, recognize patterns, and make decisions based on that knowledge. These algorithms are designed to mimic the way humans learn and reason, but they are much faster and more efficient. AI systems can process vast amounts of data in real-time, allowing them to make decisions and take actions in a fraction of the time it would take a human.

In the context of construction, AI has the potential to revolutionize the way project managers and construction managers work. By leveraging AI technologies such as machine learning and computer vision, construction professionals can automate many of the repetitive and time-consuming tasks that are involved in managing a construction project. For example, AI can be used to analyze building designs and identify potential issues before construction begins, reducing the risk of costly mistakes and delays. AI can also be used to monitor construction sites in real-time, identifying safety hazards and potential construction defects before they become major problems.

Another area where AI can have a significant impact on the construction industry is in the field of robotics. Robotics technology is advancing rapidly, and robots are becoming increasingly capable of performing tasks that were previously only possible for humans. In the construction industry, robots can be used for tasks such as bricklaying, welding, and painting, freeing up human workers to focus on more complex tasks that require human judgment and creativity.

In conclusion, AI is poised to have a major impact on the construction industry in the coming years. By leveraging AI technologies such as machine learning and robotics, construction professionals can streamline their workflows, reduce costs, and improve safety and quality on construction projects. As AI continues to evolve and mature, it will become an increasingly important tool for project managers and construction managers looking to stay ahead of the curve in this rapidly changing industry.

Overview of AI in Construction

Artificial Intelligence (AI) has been making waves across various industries, and the construction sector is no exception. In recent years, there has been a significant increase in the adoption of AI in construction, with the technology being used to enhance project management and construction processes. The integration of AI in construction has the potential to revolutionize the industry, leading to improved efficiency, cost-effectiveness, and safety.

One of the primary applications of AI in construction is in project management. AI technology can be used to predict project outcomes, identify risks and opportunities, and optimize project timelines. This helps project managers to make informed decisions and take proactive measures to prevent delays and cost overruns. AI can also assist in identifying potential safety hazards, leading to improved safety on construction sites.

Another area where AI is making a significant impact is in construction operations. The use of AI in construction equipment and machinery can help to automate tasks and optimize performance. For instance, AI-enabled drones can be used to inspect construction sites, monitor progress, and identify potential issues. Similarly, autonomous vehicles can be used to transport materials and equipment, reducing the need for human intervention.

AI is also being used to improve construction quality control. With AI-powered sensors and cameras, construction managers can monitor materials and equipment in real-time, identify defects, and ensure compliance with safety and quality standards. This leads to improved quality control and reduces the risk of defects and safety issues.

In conclusion, AI has the potential to revolutionize the construction industry, leading to improved efficiency, safety, and cost-effectiveness. Project managers and construction managers need to embrace AI technology to stay ahead of the game and remain competitive. By leveraging AI, construction companies can optimize project management, construction operations, and quality control, leading to improved project outcomes and client satisfaction.

Importance of AI in Project Management in Construction

The construction industry is one of the most complex industries in the world. It involves numerous stakeholders, including architects, engineers, contractors, subcontractors, suppliers, and clients. Managing all these stakeholders effectively is crucial for the success of any construction project. However, with the increasing complexity of construction projects, traditional project management methods are becoming less effective. This is where artificial intelligence (AI) comes in.

AI has the potential to revolutionize project management in construction. It is a powerful tool that can help project managers and construction managers to manage construction projects more efficiently and effectively. There are several ways in which AI can be used in project management in construction, including:

1. Risk management: AI can help project managers and construction managers to identify and mitigate risks in construction projects. By analyzing data from various sources, including weather forecasts, project

schedules, and financial data, AI algorithms can identify potential risks and provide recommendations to mitigate them.

2. Resource allocation: AI can help project managers and construction managers to allocate resources more effectively. By analyzing data on project schedules, resource availability, and project budgets, AI algorithms can provide recommendations on how to allocate resources to maximize productivity and minimize waste.

3. Quality control: AI can help project managers and construction managers to ensure that construction projects meet quality standards. By analyzing data on construction processes and materials, AI algorithms can identify potential quality issues and provide recommendations on how to address them.

4. Project scheduling: AI can help project managers and construction managers to optimize project schedules. By analyzing data on project tasks, dependencies, and resource availability, AI algorithms can provide recommendations on how to schedule tasks to minimize delays and maximize productivity.

In conclusion, AI is becoming increasingly important in project management in construction. It is a powerful tool that can help project managers and construction managers to manage construction projects more efficiently and effectively. By leveraging AI, construction companies can improve their project outcomes, reduce costs, and enhance their overall competitiveness in the industry.

Objectives of the Book

The objectives of this book, Artificial Intelligence for Construction: The Future of Project Management, are to provide project managers and construction managers with an in-depth understanding of artificial intelligence (AI) and how it can be applied to the construction industry. The book aims to equip readers with the knowledge and skills necessary to implement AI technology and tools to improve project management processes and outcomes.

The construction industry is known for its complex processes and challenges, such as cost overruns, schedule delays, and safety issues. These challenges can be addressed with AI technology, which can help project managers and construction managers make better decisions, optimize resources, and mitigate risks.

The book covers a variety of topics related to AI and construction, including:

1. The basics of AI and its applications in construction - The book will provide a comprehensive overview of AI technology, its

benefits, and how it can be used in the construction industry. Readers will learn about AI tools such as machine learning, natural language processing, and robotics.

2. Data management and analysis - The book will explore the importance of data in construction and how AI can be used to analyze and interpret data to inform decision-making. Readers will learn about data collection, storage, and analysis techniques.

3. Project management and scheduling - The book will examine how AI technology can be used to optimize project schedules and improve project management processes. Readers will learn about project planning, resource allocation, and risk management using AI tools.

4. Safety and risk management - The book will cover how AI technology can be used to mitigate safety risks on construction sites. Readers will learn about predictive analytics and other AI tools that can help identify potential safety hazards and prevent accidents.

5. Future trends and opportunities - The book will explore emerging trends in AI and construction, such as the use of drones and

virtual reality. Readers will gain insight into the future of AI and how it will impact the construction industry.

Overall, the objectives of this book are to provide project managers and construction managers with the knowledge and skills necessary to leverage AI technology and tools to improve project management processes and outcomes. The book will be an essential resource for anyone interested in the intersection of AI and construction.

Understanding Artificial Intelligence

What is AI?

Artificial intelligence (AI) is a branch of computer science that focuses on creating machines that can learn and perform tasks that would normally require human intelligence. AI technology is designed to perform complex operations, analyze data, make predictions, and solve problems.

The concept of AI has been around for decades, but recent advancements in machine learning, natural language processing, and robotics have made it possible for AI to be applied in a wide range of industries, including construction.

AI technology can be used to automate repetitive tasks, such as data entry and analysis, freeing up time for project managers and construction managers to focus on more important tasks. It can also be used to optimize construction processes, identify potential risks and opportunities, and improve communication and collaboration among team members.

One of the key benefits of AI technology in construction is its ability to analyze large amounts of data and provide insights that may not be immediately apparent to humans. For example, AI can analyze project data to identify patterns and trends that may indicate potential problems or opportunities for improvement.

AI can also be used to improve safety on construction sites. For example, AI- powered sensors can be used to monitor equipment and machinery for signs of wear and tear, alerting managers to potential safety concerns before they become serious issues.

In summary, AI technology has the potential to revolutionize the construction industry by automating repetitive tasks, optimizing processes, improving safety, and providing valuable insights and predictions. As project managers and construction managers, it is important to stay up to date on the latest developments in AI technology and consider how it can be applied to improve project outcomes.

Types of AI

Artificial Intelligence (AI) is a rapidly evolving technology that has the potential to revolutionize the construction industry. It is becoming increasingly relevant in the construction industry, where it has the potential to improve the efficiency, safety, and quality of construction projects. There are different types of AI that can be used in construction, including:

1. Machine Learning (ML): This type of AI uses algorithms to learn from data and make predictions or decisions. It can be used to analyze large amounts of data to identify patterns and make predictions about future events. Machine learning algorithms can be used to optimize construction processes, such as scheduling and resource allocation.

2. Natural Language Processing (NLP): This type of AI enables computers to understand and interpret human language. NLP can be used to analyze construction documents, such as contracts and specifications, to identify potential risks and opportunities.

3. Computer Vision (CV): This type of AI uses algorithms to analyze images and videos. It can be used to monitor construction sites and identify safety hazards, such as workers who are not wearing protective gear.

4. Robotics: This type of AI involves the use of robots to perform tasks that are too dangerous or difficult for humans. Robotics can be used in construction to perform tasks such as demolition, excavation, and concrete pouring.

5. Expert Systems: This type of AI uses knowledge and rules to make decisions in a specific domain. Expert systems can be used in construction to provide advice on construction methods and materials.

6. Autonomous Vehicles: This type of AI involves the use of vehicles that are capable of operating without human intervention. Autonomous vehicles can be used in construction to transport materials and equipment around construction sites.

In conclusion, AI has the potential to transform the construction industry by improving efficiency, safety, and quality. There are different types of AI that can be used in construction, including machine learning, natural language processing, computer vision, robotics, expert systems, and autonomous vehicles. Project managers and construction managers should stay up to date with the latest developments in AI and consider how they can integrate AI into their projects to improve productivity and profitability.

AI in Construction

Artificial Intelligence (AI) is revolutionizing the construction industry, transforming the way construction managers and project managers approach their work. AI can analyze vast amounts of data and provide insights that can help construction companies identify potential issues before they become problems. This can save time, money, and resources, while also improving safety and quality.

One of the key areas where AI is making a significant impact is in project management. By using AI, construction managers can better predict project timelines, identify potential areas of risk, and allocate resources more efficiently. This can help construction companies' complete projects faster and more cost-effectively, while also reducing the risk of delays and budget overruns.

AI is also being used to improve safety on construction sites. By analyzing data from sensors and cameras, AI can identify potential safety hazards and alert construction managers in real-time, allowing them to take corrective action before an accident occurs. This can help reduce the number of accidents on construction sites, making them safer for workers and reducing the risk of costly lawsuits for construction companies.

In addition to project management and safety, AI is also being used to improve the quality of construction. By analyzing data from sensors and cameras, AI can identify issues with construction materials or techniques, allowing construction managers to make corrections before they become major problems. This can help ensure that buildings are constructed to the highest standards, reducing the risk of defects, and improving the overall quality of construction.

Overall, AI is transforming the construction industry, offering new opportunities for construction managers and project managers to improve efficiency, safety, and quality. As AI continues to evolve, it is likely that we will see even more innovative applications in the construction industry, helping construction companies stay competitive and meet the demands of an increasingly complex and challenging market.

AI Applications in Project Management

Artificial Intelligence has become one of the most talked-about technologies in the construction industry today. The integration of AI in project management can automate various tasks, reduce human errors, and improve overall efficiency. With the help of AI, project managers can streamline their workflows, optimize resource allocation and scheduling, and make better decisions.

One of the most significant applications of AI in project management is in risk management. AI-powered systems can analyze data from various sources, such as weather reports, supply chain data, and project progress reports, to identify potential risks and provide recommendations to mitigate them. This can help project managers to avoid costly delays, improve safety, and reduce project risks.

Another area where AI can be useful in project management is in project scheduling. AI algorithms can analyze project data, including project tasks, resources, and timelines, and develop optimized schedules that minimize project duration and resource usage. This can help project managers to complete projects on time, within budget, and with minimal resource wastage.

AI can also be used to automate mundane and repetitive tasks, such as data entry, document management, and communication. This can free up project managers' time, allowing them to focus on more critical tasks, such as decision- making and problem-solving. AI can also help to reduce errors and improve the accuracy of data analysis.

In summary, AI has numerous applications in project management that can help project managers to improve efficiency, reduce project risks, and make better decisions. With the increasing availability of AI technologies, it is essential for project managers to keep up with the latest developments and explore how they can integrate AI into their workflows. By doing so, project managers can stay ahead of the competition and deliver successful projects that meet their clients' expectations.

The Role of AI in Construction Project Management

Benefits of AI in Construction Project Management

The construction industry is increasingly adopting artificial intelligence (AI) technology to improve planning, design, and execution of projects. AI has proven to be a valuable tool in project management, providing significant benefits to construction managers and project managers. Here are some of the benefits of AI in construction project management:

1. Improved Safety: AI can help identify safety hazards on construction sites and provide real-time alerts to workers. This helps prevent accidents and injuries, improving safety on the job site.

2. Improved Planning: AI can analyze historical data and project specifications to

help project managers plan projects more effectively. With AI, construction managers can optimize schedules, allocate resources more efficiently, and reduce project costs.

3. Increased Efficiency: AI can automate repetitive tasks, such as data entry and document management, freeing up project managers to focus on more strategic tasks. This improves the efficiency of project management, helping projects stay on track and on budget.

4. Advanced Analytics: AI can analyze large amounts of data to provide insights into construction projects. This can help project managers identify potential issues early on, allowing them to make informed decisions and take corrective action before problems arise.

5. Better Collaboration: AI can facilitate collaboration between project teams, allowing them to share information and work together more effectively. This helps reduce communication breakdowns and improves overall project performance.

6. Improved Quality Control: AI can monitor project progress and identify potential quality issues before they become significant problems. This helps ensure that projects are

completed to the highest possible standards, improving overall project quality.

In summary, AI has significant benefits for construction project management, helping to improve safety, efficiency, collaboration, and quality control. As the construction industry continues to evolve, AI will undoubtedly play an increasingly important role in project management and execution.

The Role of AI in Enhancing Planning and Scheduling

Artificial intelligence has revolutionized the way we work and live. From self-driving cars to virtual personal assistants, AI has transformed numerous industries. The construction industry is no different. With the advancement of technology, AI has emerged as a powerful tool for enhancing planning and scheduling in construction projects.

Planning and scheduling are critical components of construction project management. They involve the coordination of resources, activities, and timelines to ensure that a project is completed within budget, on time, and to the desired quality. Traditional methods of planning and scheduling involve manual processes that are time-consuming and prone to errors. This is where AI comes in.

AI can analyze vast amounts of data, identify patterns, and make predictions based on historical data. This allows project managers to make informed decisions about resource allocation, scheduling, and risk management. AI- powered tools can also help identify potential conflicts and delays before they occur, enabling project managers to take proactive measures to mitigate risks.

One of the most significant benefits of AI in planning and scheduling is its ability to optimize resource allocation. AI can analyze data on labor, equipment, and materials to identify the most efficient use of resources. This can result in significant cost savings and improved project efficiency.

Another benefit of AI in planning and scheduling is its ability to improve communication and collaboration among project stakeholders. AI-powered tools can provide real-time updates on project progress, enabling stakeholders to make informed decisions and stay informed about project status. This can lead to improved collaboration, reduced delays, and improved project outcomes.

In conclusion, AI has the potential to revolutionize planning and scheduling in construction projects. By leveraging the power of AI, project managers can optimize resource allocation, improve communication and collaboration, and mitigate risks. As AI continues to evolve, its role in construction project management will only continue to grow. It is essential for project managers to embrace this technology to stay competitive and improve project outcomes.

The Role of AI in Risk Management

The construction industry is one of the most risky and complex sectors. The success of a construction project depends on various factors, including the quality of work, cost, time, safety, and compliance. The use of artificial intelligence (AI) in risk management can help construction project managers to identify and mitigate potential risks, thereby ensuring project success.

AI can help construction project managers to analyze large data sets, such as historical project data, weather data, and site conditions, to identify potential risks. AI algorithms can quickly identify patterns and trends, which can help project managers to make informed decisions. For example, AI can help project managers to identify potential safety hazards and design flaws, which can help to prevent accidents and delays.

AI can also help project managers to monitor and track project progress in real-time. AI algorithms can analyze data from sensors, drones, and other sources to provide accurate and up-to-date information on project status. This can help project managers to identify potential delays and take corrective action before they become major issues.

AI can also help project managers to optimize project schedules and resource allocation. AI algorithms can analyze data on worker productivity, equipment usage, and other factors to identify opportunities for optimization. This can help project managers to reduce costs and improve efficiency.

Overall, the role of AI in risk management is critical in the construction industry. By leveraging AI, project managers can identify and mitigate potential risks, monitor project progress in real-time, and optimize project schedules and resource allocation. This can help construction projects to be completed on time, within budget, and with a high level of quality and safety.

The Role of AI in Resource Allocation and Management

Resource allocation and management are critical aspects of any construction project. They involve the careful planning, scheduling, and coordination of resources, including labor, materials, and equipment, to ensure that work is completed on time, within budget, and to the required quality standards. However, traditional resource allocation and management methods can be time-consuming, complex, and prone to errors.

Fortunately, advances in artificial intelligence (AI) are now providing new opportunities for project managers and construction managers to optimize resource allocation and management processes. AI technologies can help to automate and streamline many of the tasks involved in resource allocation and management, reducing the workload, and freeing up time for more strategic decision-making.

One of the key benefits of AI in resource allocation and management is its ability to analyze large amounts of data quickly and accurately. For example, AI algorithms can use historical project data to identify patterns and trends in resource usage, allowing project managers to forecast future resource needs with greater accuracy. This can help to ensure that resources are allocated more efficiently, reducing waste, and minimizing delays.

AI can also help to optimize the scheduling of resources. By analyzing data on project timelines, resource availability, and other factors, AI algorithms can generate optimal schedules that take into account all relevant constraints and factors. This can help to ensure that resources are used efficiently, and that work is completed on time.

In addition to improving resource allocation and scheduling, AI can also help to improve the management of resources during construction projects. For example, AI-powered sensors and monitoring systems can be used to track the location, usage, and condition of equipment and materials in real-time. This can help to reduce theft, loss, and damage, and ensure that resources are being used effectively.

Overall, the role of AI in resource allocation and management is becoming increasingly important in the construction industry. By leveraging AI technologies, project managers and construction managers can optimize resource allocation and management processes, reduce costs, and improve project outcomes. As such, it is essential for professionals in the construction industry to stay up to date with the latest developments in AI and to explore how these technologies can be applied to their work.

AI Applications in Construction Project Management

AI for Project Planning and Design

Artificial Intelligence (AI) is transforming the construction industry, and project planning and design are no exceptions. With AI, project managers and construction managers can optimize their planning and design processes, reduce risks, and increase efficiency. In this subchapter, we will explore how AI can be used for project planning and design, its benefits, and its challenges.

AI can help project managers and construction managers in the following ways:

1. Predictive analysis: AI can analyze data from past projects and predict the outcome of similar projects. This can help project managers and construction managers to anticipate potential risks and take preventive measures.

2. Optimization: AI can optimize project schedules, resource allocation, and cost estimates. This can help project managers

and construction managers to minimize costs and maximize efficiency.

3. Simulation: AI can simulate different scenarios and provide insights into the impact of design decisions. This can help project managers and construction managers to make informed decisions and avoid costly mistakes.

4. Collaboration: AI can facilitate collaboration among project stakeholders, such as architects, engineers, and contractors. This can help project managers and construction managers to ensure that everyone is on the same page and reduce the risk of miscommunication.

The benefits of AI for project planning and design are numerous. It can help project managers and construction managers to save time and money, reduce risks, and increase efficiency. However, there are also challenges that need to be addressed. These include:

1. Data quality: AI relies on data, and if the data is of poor quality, the results will be inaccurate. Project managers and construction managers need to ensure that the data they use for AI analysis is accurate and up to date.

2. Integration: AI needs to be integrated into existing project management and construction management systems. This can be challenging, especially if the systems are outdated or incompatible with AI.

3. Training: Project managers and construction managers need to be trained in AI to use it effectively. This can be time-consuming and costly.

In conclusion, AI is transforming the way project planning and design are done in the construction industry. It has the potential to revolutionize the industry and make project management and construction management more efficient, cost-effective, and less risky. However, to fully realize the benefits of AI, project managers and construction managers need to address the challenges and invest in the necessary resources and training.

AI for Construction Site Management

Artificial Intelligence (AI) is quickly becoming an essential tool in the construction industry, revolutionizing how project managers and construction managers handle site management. With AI, construction managers can now easily track the progress of their projects, monitor site safety, and optimize resources to ensure that projects are completed on time, within budget, and to the highest quality standards. In this subchapter, we'll explore how AI is transforming construction site management and the benefits it provides to project managers and construction managers.

One of the significant benefits of AI for construction site management is the ability to monitor and analyze site data in real-time. With sensors and cameras installed on construction sites, AI algorithms can gather and process valuable data on worker productivity, equipment usage, and site safety. This data can then be used to make informed decisions in real-time, allowing project managers to address issues promptly and optimize resource allocation.

Another area where AI is transforming construction site management is in site safety. With AI-powered cameras and sensors, construction managers can now monitor site safety in real-time, identifying potential hazards and alerting workers immediately. AI can also analyze data on worker behavior and identify patterns that could lead to accidents, allowing managers to implement targeted safety training programs.

AI is also transforming resource management in construction. With AI algorithms, project managers can optimize resource allocation, ensuring that equipment and workers are utilized efficiently. This can lead to cost savings, as projects are completed faster and with fewer resources.

In conclusion, AI is transforming construction site management in various ways, providing project managers and construction managers with real-time data, improved site safety, and optimized resource allocation. As AI technology continues to evolve, we can expect to see even more changes in how construction sites are managed, leading to faster, safer, and more efficient projects.

AI for Quality Control and Monitoring

Quality control has always been a critical aspect of construction management. The quality of a construction project can make or break its success, and construction managers must ensure that their projects meet the highest standards of quality. In the past, quality control was a manual process that required a lot of time and effort. However, with the advent of artificial intelligence (AI), quality control has become more efficient and effective.

AI can be used in quality control in several ways. One of the most common applications of AI in quality control is using machine learning algorithms. These algorithms can analyze large amounts of data and identify patterns and anomalies that may indicate quality issues. For example, AI can be used to analyze data from sensors and other monitoring devices to detect changes in temperature, humidity, and other environmental factors that may affect the quality of a construction project.

Another way that AI can be used in quality control is using computer vision. Computer vision is a technology that allows computers to interpret and analyze images and videos. This technology can be used to detect defects and other quality issues in construction projects. For example, computer vision can be used to analyze images of concrete surfaces to detect cracks and other defects that may indicate quality issues.

AI can also be used in quality control to monitor construction processes in real- time. This can be done using sensors and other monitoring devices that can capture data on various aspects of the construction process, such as temperature, humidity, and vibration. This data can then be analyzed in real- time to detect issues and take corrective action before they become major problems.

In conclusion, AI has a lot of potential in quality control and monitoring in construction. By leveraging the power of AI, construction managers can ensure that their projects meet the highest standards of quality and avoid costly delays and rework. While AI is still in its early stages in construction, itis clear that it will play an increasingly important role in the future of project management.

AI for Predictive Maintenance

Predictive maintenance is crucial in the construction industry, where equipment downtime can lead to project delays and increased costs. AI can play a significant role in predicting equipment failures and scheduling maintenance activities proactively.

Using AI, project managers and construction managers can analyze equipment data and identify patterns that indicate potential equipment failures. The AI algorithms can also learn from historical data and predict when maintenance activities are required.

The benefits of using AI for predictive maintenance in construction are numerous. It can help reduce equipment downtime and increase the lifespan of equipment. It can also improve safety by identifying potential hazards before they occur.

One example of AI for predictive maintenance in construction is the use of sensors that collect data from equipment. This data can be analyzed using AI algorithms to predict when maintenance is required. This not only saves time but also reduces costs by avoiding unnecessary maintenance activities.

Another example is the use of AI-powered drones for inspection activities. Drones equipped with cameras and sensors can capture data on the condition of equipment and infrastructure. This data can be analyzed using AI algorithms to identify potential issues and schedule maintenance activities proactively.

Overall, AI for predictive maintenance in construction has the potential to revolutionize the industry by reducing downtime, improving safety, and increasing efficiency. Project managers and construction managers should embrace this technology to stay ahead of the curve and ensure the success of their projects.

Challenges of Implementing AI in Construction

Legal and Ethical Issues

The implementation of artificial intelligence (AI) in construction has opened a new era of efficiency and productivity for the industry. However, as with any technological advancement, there are legal and ethical issues that need to be addressed to ensure that the use of AI in construction is safe and fair for all parties involved.

One of the primary legal concerns when it comes to AI in construction is liability. Who is responsible if an AI system makes a mistake that leads to damage or injury? Is it the construction company, the software provider, or both? The answer will depend on the specific circumstances of the incident, but it is essential for construction managers to be aware of the potential risks and to have a plan in place to mitigate them.

Another legal issue is data privacy. AI systems require access to vast amounts of data to function effectively, and this data often includes sensitive information about individuals and companies. It is essential to ensure that this data is protected, and that the AI system is only using it for the intended purpose. Failure to do so could result in legal action and damage to the company's reputation.

The ethical concerns surrounding AI in construction are equally important. One of the most pressing ethical issues is the potential for AI to replace human workers. While AI can perform many tasks more efficiency than humans, it is essential to consider the impact on the workforce and to ensure that workers are not unfairly displaced.

Another ethical concern is bias. AI systems are only as unbiased as the data they are trained on, and if this data is biased, the AI will be too. This could lead to unfair treatment of certain groups of people, such as women or minorities. Construction managers need to ensure that AI systems are trained on unbiased data and that any potential biases are identified and addressed.

In conclusion, the use of AI in construction has the potential to revolutionize the industry. However, it is essential to address legal and ethical issues to ensure that the use of AI is safe and fair for all parties involved. Construction managers need to be aware of these issues and to have a plan in place to mitigate any potential risks. By doing so, they can reap the benefits of AI without compromising on safety or ethics.

Data Management and Security

With the increasing use of AI in construction, data management and security are becoming critical issues for project managers and construction managers. AI algorithms require large amounts of data to function properly, which means that data management and security are essential for the successful implementation of AI in construction.

Data Management

Data management is the process of collecting, storing, processing, and analyzing data to gain insights into the construction project. AI algorithms are only as effective as the data they are trained on, so it is essential to ensure that the data is accurate, relevant, and up to date.

One of the main challenges in data management is the fragmentation of data across different systems and platforms. Construction projects involve multiple stakeholders and parties, each with their own systems and data sources. This fragmentation makes it challenging to integrate and analyze data effectively.

To overcome this challenge, project managers and construction managers should adopt a holistic approach to data management. This approach involves using a centralized data platform that can integrate data from different sources and provide a single source of truth for the project.

Security

Data security is a critical issue in the construction industry, particularly with the increasing use of AI. Construction projects involve sensitive information such as financial data, project plans, and intellectual property. This information must be protected from unauthorized access, theft, and cyber-attacks.

To ensure data security, project managers and construction managers should adopt a multi-layered approach to security. This approach involves using a combination of physical, technical, and administrative controls to protect the data.

Physical controls include measures such as access control systems, surveillance cameras, and physical barriers to prevent unauthorized physical access to the data.

Technical controls include measures such as encryption, firewalls, and intrusion detection systems to protect the data from unauthorized access over the network.

Administrative controls include policies and procedures such as access control policies, data retention policies, and incident response plans to ensure that the data is managed and protected effectively.

Conclusion

Data management and security are critical issues for project managers and construction managers in the age of AI. Adopting a holistic approach to data management and a multi-layered approach to data security can help ensure the successful implementation of AI in construction projects.

Integration with Existing Systems

One of the biggest challenges that project managers and construction managers face when implementing artificial intelligence in construction is integrating these technologies with existing systems. Construction projects are incredibly complex and involve many stakeholders, each with their own set of tools and processes. As a result, integrating new technologies can be a daunting task.

However, it is essential to integrate AI with existing systems to ensure that these technologies can deliver their full potential. Here are some tips for successfully integrating AI into your construction projects.

1. Identify the Gaps

The first step in integrating AI with existing systems is to identify the gaps in your current processes. This involves evaluating your current systems and processes and identifying areas where AI can help improve efficiency, productivity, and accuracy. This can include everything from project planning and scheduling to quality control and safety monitoring.

2. Choose the Right AI Tools

Once you have identified the gaps in your processes, the next step is to choose the right AI tools to address those gaps. There are a variety of AI technologies available in the market, each with its unique features and capabilities. It is essential to select the right tools that align with your project goals and requirements.

3. Ensure Compatibility

Before integrating AI with existing systems, it is crucial to ensure compatibility between the two. This involves evaluating your current systems and processes to identify any potential conflicts or issues that could arise during integration. It is essential to work closely with your AI vendor to ensure that their technology is compatible with your existing systems.

4. Train Your Team

Integrating AI with existing systems involves a significant change in your processes and workflows. It is essential to train your team on how to use the new technology effectively. This involves providing training and support to your team members to ensure that they are comfortable using the new tools.

5. Monitor and Evaluate

Finally, it is essential to monitor and evaluate the effectiveness of your AI integration. This involves tracking key metrics such as productivity, efficiency, and accuracy to ensure that the new technology is delivering the desired results. It is also crucial to gather feedback from your team members to identify any issues or areas for improvement.

In conclusion, integrating AI with existing systems is a complex process that requires careful planning, evaluation, and execution. By following the tips mentioned above, project managers and construction managers can successfully integrate AI into their workflows and improve project outcomes.

Cost of Implementation

The implementation of Artificial Intelligence (AI) in construction projects involves a range of costs, and Project and Construction Managers need to be aware of them. The costs of implementation can be categorized into two main types: direct and indirect costs.

Direct Costs

Direct costs are the expenses that are directly associated with the implementation of AI in construction projects. These costs may include the purchase of hardware and software, installation and configuration, and training and development of personnel.

Hardware and Software

The first and most significant direct cost is the purchase of hardware and software. To implement AI in construction projects, companies need to invest in computer hardware and software that can support the technology. The hardware requirements may include high-performance servers, powerful graphics cards, and storage devices. The software requirements may include AI engines, machine learning algorithms, and data analysis tools.

Installation and Configuration

The installation and set-up of AI hardware and software is another direct cost. Companies may need to hire IT professionals to install and configure the AI systems. This process may also involve network upgrades, security protocols, and data integration.

Training and Development

The final direct cost is the training and development of personnel. Employees need to be trained on how to use the AI systems effectively. This training may involve classroom instruction, online courses, and hands-on experience. Companies may also need to hire new personnel with specialized skills in AI and data analysis.

Indirect Costs

Indirect costs are the expenses that are not directly associated with the implementation of AI in construction projects but may still impact the budget. These costs may include downtime, maintenance, and data management.

Downtime

Downtime is an indirect cost that may occur during the installation and configuration of AI systems. During this process, operations may need to be disrupted, and employees may need to be relocated. This downtime may result in lost productivity and revenue.

Maintenance

Maintenance is another indirect cost associated with AI implementation. AI systems require regular maintenance to ensure they are functioning correctly. This maintenance may involve software updates, hardware upgrades, and system testing.

Data Management

Finally, data management is an indirect cost that needs to be considered. AI systems generate vast amounts of data that need to be stored, analyzed, and maintained. The cost of data management may include the purchase of storage devices, data analysis tools, and personnel to manage data.

Conclusion

The cost of implementing AI in construction projects is significant and involves direct and indirect costs. Project and Construction Managers need to be aware of these costs and factor them into their budgets. The benefits of AI, however, are equally significant and include increased productivity, improved safety, and reduced costs in the long run. By carefully weighing the costs and benefits of AI implementation, Project and Construction Managers can make informed decisions that improve their projects' overall performance.

The Future of AI in Construction

Trends in AI Development for Construction

Artificial intelligence (AI) has transformative potential in the construction industry by streamlining processes, reducing costs, and improving safety on job sites. As construction projects continue to grow in complexity, AI is helping project managers and construction managers to stay ahead of the curve. Here are some of the latest trends in AI development for construction:

1. Autonomous equipment

Construction companies are investing in autonomous equipment to increase efficiency and safety. For example, self-driving bulldozers, excavators, and trucks can work around the clock without a break. These machines can also be programmed to avoid obstacles and adjust for unforeseen circumstances.

2. Predictive analytics

Predictive analytics is a type of AI that uses historical data to make predictions about future events. In construction, predictive analytics can be used to forecast project timelines, material costs, and potential risks. This allows project managers to make informed decisions and avoid delays and budget overruns.

3. Chatbots and virtual assistants

Chatbots and virtual assistants can help construction companies improve communication and productivity. These AI-powered assistants can answer common questions, provide updates on project status, and even help with scheduling and coordination.

4. Computer vision

Computer vision is an AI technology that allows computers to interpret and understand images and video. In construction, computer vision can be used to monitor job sites for safety violations, track progress, and identify potential hazards.

5. Machine learning

Machine learning is a type of AI that allows computers to learn from data without being explicitly programmed. In construction, machine learning can be used to optimize building designs, predict maintenance needs, and improve safety protocols.

6. Drones

Drones are becoming increasingly popular in construction as they allow for aerial surveys, inspections, and mapping. With AI, drones can automatically identify and ag potential issues, such as cracks in a building's foundation or damage to a roof.

In conclusion, AI is transforming the construction industry and helping project managers and construction managers to work more efficiently, safely, and cost- effectively. By keeping up with the latest trends in AI development for construction, companies can stay ahead of the curve and reap the benefits of this transformative technology.

The construction industry has always been one of the most labor-intensive and time-consuming industries, but with the advent of artificial intelligence (AI), the sector is set to experience a significant transformation. AI is a game- changing technology that has the potential to revolutionize the way construction project management is carried out. As AI continues to evolve, it is becoming increasingly clear that it is going to play a critical role in shaping the future of construction.

The integration of AI into construction project management has the potential to transform the way projects are planned, executed, and monitored. Some of the areas where AI can have an impact include project planning, risk management, scheduling, and resource allocation. AI can analyze data and provide insights that can help project managers make informed decisions, reducing the risk of errors and delays.

One of the most exciting benefits of AI in construction project management is the ability to identify potential risks and take proactive measures to mitigate them. AI algorithms can analyze data from past construction projects, identify patterns, and predict potential risks. This information can help project managers make informed decisions about the best course of action to take.

AI can also help with scheduling and resource allocation. With AI algorithms, project managers can optimize schedules to ensure that resources are allocated optimally. This can help reduce costs and improve project timelines. AI can also help with the identification of critical path activities, allowing project managers to prioritize tasks and ensure that resources are allocated appropriately.

Another area where AI can be beneficial in construction project management is the monitoring of project progress. AI algorithms can analyze data in real-time and provide project managers with insights into project status, helping them make informed decisions about the best course of action.

In conclusion, the integration of AI into construction project management is set to transform the industry. By leveraging AI technology, project managers can optimize project planning, risk management, scheduling, and resource allocation, leading to improved project outcomes. As AI continues to evolve, it will play an increasingly critical role in shaping the future of construction.

Opportunities for Innovation and Growth

Artificial intelligence has been making waves in the construction industry, and it's not hard to see why. AI has the potential to revolutionize many aspects of construction management, from safety and quality control to project scheduling and cost estimation. In this chapter, we'll explore some of the opportunities for innovation and growth that AI presents to project managers and construction managers.

One of the most exciting areas of AI in construction is predictive analytics. By analyzing historical data and real-time information from sensors and other sources, AI can help project managers predict and mitigate risks before they become major issues. For example, AI can analyze weather data to help construction managers make decisions about whether to proceed with outdoor work or delay it due to inclement weather. It can also analyze data from equipment and sensors to identify potential equipment failures before they happen, reducing downtime and increasing productivity.

Another area where AI can make a big impact is in project scheduling. By analyzing historical data and using machine learning algorithms, AI can help project managers create more accurate schedules that consider factors such as weather, site conditions, and resource availability. This can help reduce delays and cost overruns, as well as improve overall project efficiency.

AI can also help improve safety on construction sites. By analyzing data from sensors and cameras, AI can identify potential hazards and alert workers to potential dangers. It can also analyze data from wearables and other sources to monitor worker health and well-being, helping to prevent accidents and injuries.

Cost estimation is another area where AI can help construction managers. By analyzing historical data and using machine learning algorithms, AI can help project managers create more accurate cost estimates that consider factors such as material costs, labor costs, and other expenses. This can help reduce cost overruns and improve overall project profitability.

In conclusion, AI presents many opportunities for innovation and growth in the construction industry. From predictive analytics and project scheduling to safety monitoring and cost estimation, AI can help project managers and construction managers make better decisions and improve overall project efficiency and profitability. As AI technology continues to evolve, it's exciting to think about the new ways it will transform construction management in the years to come.

Challenges to Overcome

Artificial Intelligence (is transforming the construction industry and revolutionizing project management. However, the integration of AI into the construction process is not without its challenges. As project managers and construction managers navigate the adoption of AI, they must address a range of obstacles to ensure the successful implementation of the technology.

One of the primary challenges to overcome is the resistance to change. The construction industry has been slow to embrace technology, and many workers may be hesitant to accept AI to improve their workflows Project managers must take a proactive approach to educate workers on the benefits of AI and how it can streamline their work, reduce errors, and improve safety.

Another challenge is the lack of data. AI relies on data to learn and make decisions, but construction projects often have limited data sets. Project managers must work with their teams to gather and input data to teach AI algorithms and help them make accurate predictions.

AI also requires considerable computing power, which can be a challenge for some construction firms. Project managers should explore cloud-based solutions, which can provide the necessary resources to run AI algorithms without investing in expensive hardware.

Additionally, AI may not be a one-size-fits-all solution. The construction industry is highly diverse, with a wide range of projects, materials, and equipment. Project managers must carefully evaluate their specific needs and determine which AI applications will be most effective for their projects.

Finally, there are ethical concerns surrounding the use of AI in construction. As AI algorithms make decisions, there is a risk of bias or discrimination. Project managers must ensure that their AI systems are transparent, explainable, and accountable, to avoid unintended consequences.

In conclusion, while AI offer tremendous potential to improve project management and construction processes, there are challenges to overcome. Project managers must be proactive in addressing these challenges to ensure the successful adoption of AI in the construction industry. By educating workers, gathering data, exploring cloud-based solutions, evaluating specific needs, and addressing ethical concerns, the construction industry can harness the power of AI to drive innovation and improve outcomes.

Case Studies

Artificial Intelligence for Construction Site Monitoring

One of the most promising applications of AI in construction is site monitoring. The traditional approach to monitoring construction sites is time-consuming, labor-intensive, and prone to errors. However, with the help of AI, construction managers can now monitor their sites in real-time and make data-driven decisions that can help them save time, money and improve safety.

To illustrate the potential of AI for construction site monitoring, let's look at a case study.

Case Study 1: AI for Construction Site Monitoring

The project in question is a high-rise building that was under construction in a busy urban area. The construction site was challenging to manage due to several factors such as limited space, high traffic, and multiple stakeholders involved. The construction manager wanted to ensure that the project was on track, and any issues were addressed promptly to avoid delays and cost overruns.

The construction manager decided to deploy an AI-powered site monitoring system that used drones and cameras to capture data in real-time. The system was connected to a cloud-based platform that used machine learning algorithms to analyze the data and provide insights to the construction manager.

The system monitored several aspects of the construction site, such as progress, safety, and quality. The drones captured images and videos of the site, which were analyzed by the machine learning algorithms to generate reports on the progress of the project. The system also used computer vision to detect safety hazards such as workers not wearing helmets or standing in dangerous areas.

The construction manager could access the reports from the platform anytime and make data-driven decisions to improve the project's performance. For instance, if the system detected a delay in the progress of a particular task, the construction manager could allocate more resources to that task to ensure it was completed on time.

The AI-powered site monitoring system proved to be a game-changer for the construction manager. The system helped them save time, reduce costs, and improve safety. The construction manager could make data-driven decisions that resulted in a more efficient construction process, and the project was completed on time and within budget.

Conclusion

AI-powered site monitoring systems have the potential to transform the construction industry by providing real-time insights that can help construction managers make data-driven decisions. The case study we have discussed demonstrates how AI can help construction managers monitor their sites more efficiently, improve safety and reduce costs. As AI technology continues to evolve, we can expect to see more innovative applications of AI in construction project management.

Case Study 2: AI for Predictive Maintenance

In recent years, the use of AI in the construction industry has been gaining traction. One area where AI has been highly effective is in predictive maintenance. Predictive maintenance is the use of data analytics and machine learning algorithms to predict when equipment or machinery is likely to fail. By doing so, it allows for maintenance to be performed proactively, reducing the likelihood of costly downtime and repairs.

A prime example of AI for predictive maintenance in action is the construction of the new World Trade Center in New York City. As part of the construction process, a team of engineers and data scientists were tasked with developing a predictive maintenance system for the elevators in the building. Using data from sensors placed throughout the elevators, the team was able to train machine learning algorithms to predict when an elevator was likely to fail. By doing so, they were able to schedule maintenance proactively, reducing downtime and ensuring the optimal operation of the elevators.

Another example of AI for predictive maintenance in construction is the use of drones for building inspections. Drones equipped with high-resolution cameras and sensors can be used to inspect buildings for damage or wear and tear. Using AI algorithms, the data collected by the drones can be analyzed to predict when repairs or maintenance will be required. This allows for building owners and managers to schedule maintenance proactively, reducing costly repairs and downtime.

AI for predictive maintenance has also been used in the construction of wind turbines. Wind turbines are subject to a great deal of wear and tear, and maintenance can be costly and time-consuming. Using data from sensors placed throughout the turbines, AI algorithms can be trained to predict when maintenance is required. This allows for maintenance to be scheduled proactively, reducing downtime, and ensuring the efficient operation of the turbines.

In conclusion, AI for predictive maintenance has shown great promise in the construction industry. By analyzing data from sensors and using machine learning algorithms, predictive maintenance systems can predict when equipment or machinery is likely to fail. This allows for maintenance to be performed proactively, reducing downtime, and ensuring the efficient operation of construction projects.

Case Study 3: AI for Quality Control and Monitoring

In the construction industry, ensuring the quality of materials and workmanship is crucial to the success of a project. However, traditional methods of quality control and monitoring can be time-consuming and prone to human error. Artificial intelligence (AI) presents a solution to this problem, by providing real-time analysis and insights that can help project managers and construction managers make informed decisions.

One example of AI for quality control and monitoring is the use of drones equipped with sensors and cameras. These drones can y over construction sites and capture data on various aspects of the project, such as the quality of materials and the progress of work. The data is then analyzed using machine learning algorithms to identify any potential issues or areas that require attention. This enables project managers to take proactive measures to address these issues before they become major problems.

Another example is the use of AI-powered software to monitor the quality of materials. This software can analyze data from sensors installed in materials such as concrete, steel, and wood, and identify any anomalies or defects that could compromise the structural integrity of the building. This allows project managers to take corrective action before the issue becomes a safety hazard.

AI can also help with monitoring the performance of equipment and machinery on construction sites. By analyzing data from sensors installed on equipment, AI can identify any potential issues or maintenance needs before they cause downtime or other problems. This can help project managers optimize the use of equipment and reduce costs associated with maintenance and repairs.

In summary, AI has the potential to revolutionize quality control and monitoring in the construction industry. By providing real-time analysis and insights, AI can help project managers and construction managers make informed decisions, optimize the use of resources, and ensure the safety and quality of construction projects. As the technology continues to evolve, we can expect to see even more innovative applications of AI in construction.

Conclusion

Summary of the Book

Artificial Intelligence for Construction: The Future of Project Management is a book that provides a comprehensive overview of how AI is transforming the construction industry. The book is addressed towards project managers and construction managers who are interested in learning about the benefits of incorporating AI into their projects.

The book begins by introducing the concept of AI and how it is being used in various industries. The authors then delve into the application of artificial intelligence in the construction industry, highlighting its potential to improve project management, safety, and productivity.

The book discusses several key areas where AI can be applied in construction, including scheduling, cost estimation, quality control, and risk management. The authors provide detailed examples of how AI can be used to automate these processes, reduce errors, and improve overall project outcomes.

In addition to discussing the benefits of artificial intelligence in construction, the book also addresses some of the challenges and concerns associated with its implementation. The authors acknowledge that while AI has the potential to revolutionize the construction industry, there are also ethical and social considerations that must be considered. The book provides guidance on how to navigate these issues and ensure that artificial intelligence is used in a responsible and ethical manner.

Overall, Artificial Intelligence for Construction: The Future of Project Management is an essential guide for project managers and construction managers who are interested in learning more about the benefits of incorporating AI into their projects. The book provides a clear and concise overview of how artificial intelligence can be applied in construction, as well as guidance on how to navigate the challenges and concerns associated with its implementation. With the insights and recommendations provided in this book, project managers and construction managers can leverage artificial intelligence to improve their projects, increase productivity, and stay ahead of the competition.

Final Thoughts on AI in Construction Project Management

As the construction industry continues to evolve, it is essential to embrace new technologies that can help improve project management processes. One of the most promising tools that have emerged in recent years is artificial intelligence (AI).

AI has the potential to revolutionize the construction industry by improving efficiency, reducing costs, and enhancing safety. In project management, AI can be used to automate routine tasks, analyze data, and provide insights that can help managers make better decisions.

One of the main benefits of AI in construction project management is that it can help reduce errors and improve accuracy. By automating tasks such as scheduling, cost estimation, and risk assessment, AI can help ensure that projects are completed on time and within budget.

Another benefit of AI is that it can help construction managers analyze data more effectively. By collecting data from various sources such as sensors, drones, and other devices, AI can provide insights into project performance, identify areas for improvement, and help managers make data-driven decisions.

However, it is important to note that AI is not a replacement for human expertise. While AI can help automate routine tasks and provide insights, it still requires human input and oversight to ensure that projects are completed successfully.

Furthermore, AI can also raise ethical concerns, such as biases in algorithms or potential job displacement. Construction managers must be aware of these issues and take steps to address them appropriately.

In conclusion, AI has the potential to transform the construction industry by improving project management processes. However, it is important to use AI appropriately and with caution, considering ethical concerns and the need for human expertise. By embracing AI and other new technologies, construction managers can stay ahead of the curve and achieve greater success in their projects.

Recommendations for Further Research

The use of AI in construction has been growing rapidly in recent years. As the technology continues to evolve, there are many areas where further research could help to improve the use of AI in construction project management. Here are a few recommendations for areas that could benefit from additional research:

1. Integration of AI with Building Information Modeling (BIM)

BIM is a powerful tool for construction project management that allows for the creation of detailed 3D models of buildings and structures. AI can be used to further enhance the capabilities of BIM, such as automating the identification of potential construction issues or optimizing project scheduling. Further research could help to identify the most effective ways to integrate AI with BIM and how it can improve overall project management.

2. Risk assessment and mitigation using AI

Construction projects are inherently risky, with many factors that can impact the success of a project. AI can be used to analyze various data points, such as weather patterns and previous project data, to identify potential risks and develop mitigation strategies. Further research could help to identify the most effective ways to use AI for risk assessment and mitigation in construction projects.

3. AI for equipment and resource management

Construction projects require a tremendous amount of equipment and resources, and managing these effectively is critical to project success. AI can be used to optimize resource allocation and equipment usage, reducing waste, and improving efficiency. Further research could help to identify the most effective ways to use AI for equipment and resource management in construction projects.

4. Predictive maintenance using AI

Construction equipment is subject to wear and tear, and breakdowns can cause delays and cost overruns. AI can be used to analyze data from equipment sensors and predict when maintenance is required, helping to prevent breakdowns and optimize maintenance schedules. Further research could help to identify the most effective ways to use AI for predictive maintenance in construction projects.

Overall, there are many areas where further research could help to improve the use of AI in construction project management. By continuing to explore these areas, we can unlock the full potential of AI and drive greater efficiency and success in construction projects.

Glossary

Definition of Key Terms and Concepts

When delving into the topic of artificial intelligence (AI) for construction, it is important to have a clear understanding of the key terms and concepts involved. Here, we will define some of the most common terms and concepts that will be referenced throughout the book.

Artificial Intelligence (AI)

AI refers to the ability of machines to perform tasks that typically require human intelligence, such as learning, problem-solving, decision-making, and natural language processing. AI systems use algorithms and statistical models to analyze data and make predictions or decisions based on that analysis.

Machine Learning (ML)

ML is a subset of AI that focuses on the ability of machines to learn from data and improve their performance over time without being explicitly programmed. ML algorithms use statistical models to identify patterns and make predictions based on those patterns.

Deep Learning (DL)

DL is a subset of ML that uses neural networks – layered networks of artificial neurons – to learn from large amounts of data. DL algorithms can be used for tasks such as image and speech recognition, natural language processing, and autonomous driving.

Internet of Things (IoT)

IoT refers to the network of physical devices, vehicles, buildings, and other objects that are embedded with sensors, software, and connectivity to enable them to collect and exchange data. IoT devices can be used to monitor and control various aspects of construction projects, such as temperature, humidity, and energy usage.

Robotics

Robotics refers to the design, construction, and operation of robots – machines that can perform tasks autonomously or under remote control. Robotics technology can be used in construction for tasks such as excavation, demolition, and material handling.

Digital Twin

A digital twin is a virtual replica of a physical asset, such as a building or a machine. Digital twins can be used to simulate and analyze the performance of the physical asset in real-time, allowing for predictive maintenance and optimization.

In conclusion, understanding these key terms and concepts is crucial for any project manager or construction manager looking to incorporate AI into their operations. By having a clear understanding of these concepts, professionals can better understand the potential benefits and limitations of AI in construction and make informed decisions about its implementation.

References
List of Sources Cited in the Book

List of Sources Cited in the Book

As the field of artificial intelligence continues to evolve, it is essential to keep up with the latest research and developments. This book has drawn from a variety of sources to provide a comprehensive overview of how AI is transforming the construction industry, and the following is a list of some of the most important works cited.

1. "Artificial Intelligence in Construction: A Systematic Review," by Seyedehzahra Mirrahimi, Hadi Meftahi, and Amirhossein Taherkhani. This paper provides a thorough review of the literature on AI in construction, summarizing the key findings and identifying areas for further research.

2. "The Impact of Artificial Intelligence on Project Management," by John P. Biedermann. This article explores how AI is changing the way project managers work and provides insights into the benefits and challenges of using AI in project management.

3. "Construction Robotics and Automation: An Overview of the Current State of the Art," by

Thomas Bock and Thomas Linner. This book chapter provides an in- depth overview of the latest developments in construction robotics and automation, including AI-powered machines and systems.

4. "Deep Learning for Visual Understanding in the Construction Industry," by Jie Zhang, Hongqiao Liu, and Jianhong Huang. This paper discusses how deep learning algorithms can be used to analyze images and video data in construction, improving safety and efficiency on job sites.

5. "Machine Learning for Predictive Maintenance of Construction Equipment," by Jakub Mościcki, Marcin Kacprzak, and Paweł Stefaniak. This article describes how machine learning can be used to predict equipment failures and reduce downtime on construction sites.

6. "Intelligent Planning and Scheduling for Construction Projects," by Ghang Lee and Tarek Zayed. This book chapter explores how AI-powered planning and scheduling tools can help construction managers optimize resources and reduce project timelines.

7. "A Review of Machine Learning Applications in Construction," by Mahendran

Kandasamy, Negar El-Hamamsy, and S. Thomas Ng. This paper provides a comprehensive overview of how machine learning is being used in construction, from predicting project outcomes to optimizing supply chain management.

These are just a few of the many sources cited in this book, which aims to provide a comprehensive overview of how AI is transforming the construction industry. By drawing on the latest research and insights from experts in the field, this book covers valuable insights for project managers and construction managers looking to stay ahead of the curve.

Made in the USA
Monee, IL
12 June 2023